The General Care and Maintenance
of
True Chameleons
Part I Husbandry

by Philippe de Vosjoli

Table of Contents

Introduction

Within the last ten years, major breakthroughs developed in the field of herpetoculture, which have resulted in improved care and increasing succes in the long term maintenance and propagation of reptiles.

As a result, species once considered difficult to keep alive are being maintained successfully by devoted herpetoculturists both in zoological institutions and the private sector.

This book was written from the point of view of a herpetoculturist with the goal of making practical herpetocultural information available to the general public as well as more experienced herpetoculturists. Thus, its emphasis is to provide information on captive care rather than the herpetology of chameleons, an area which is beyond the scope and intention of this book.

In the late 1970's the author worked for two unique people, Susan and Vern French, in a little store in upper east side Manhattan called Small Worlds. This store promoted a concept which to this day can be considered avant guard in the United States; European-style naturalistic vivaria that, unlike most reptile displays seen in pet stores, looked attractive enough that you would proudly display one of these units in your office or living room. The store advocated large vivaria with natural plants, full spectrum lighting, fans for ventilation and directional heat sources. Eventually, Susan and Vern's interest focused on true chameleons with varying amounts of failure and success. The greatest failures were due to inadequate information on temperature requirements and lack of information on the critical role of internal parasites in these animals. Successes included the indoor rearing of newborn Jackson's chameleons to near maturity and the successful maintenance of several species for relatively long periods of time. During this process, significant information was gathered on the requirements of various species and on diseases and their possible treatment.

As a result of his employment with Small Worlds, the author eventually became involved with a well intended organization called the Chameleon Research Center (CRC) whose primary goals were to determine methods for the captive husbandry and propagation of chameleons. The greatest flaw of the CRC was publishing a journal without ever editing or correcting or submitting a pre-publication copy to the initial authors and the director for correction and review. The results were publications (including this author's) which had valuable content while being riddled with embarassing typos, omissions and misspellings. The information presented in this book is the result of those experiences and of the author's current research with chameleons and other lizard species.

This book is dedicated to Susan French who eventually became Susan Jones. If she were alive today I think she would have been pleased with this little book.

General Information

Female Parson's chameleon *(Chamaeleo parsoni)*.

True chameleons are members of the Old World family Chamaeleontidae. These are unrelated to the species commonly sold in the pet trade under the names of chameleons or American chameleons which should properly be called anoles and that belong to the New World genus *Anolis* in the family Iguanidae.

There are approximately 85 recognized species of true chameleons placed in the genera *Chamaeleo* (approximately 65 species) and *Brookesia* (approximately 20 species). Some herpetologists have further broken down the genus *Chamaeleo* into subgenera. The former genera *Leandria* and *Evoluticauda* from Madagascar are now considered to be members of the genus *Brookesia* .

This book focuses on the care of members of the genus *Chamaeleo* since *Brookesia* , at the time of writing, are virtually unavailable in the herpetocultural trade.

3

DISTRIBUTION

True chameleons are found in Africa and Madagascar with one species, *Chamaeleo chamaeleon*, also found in Southern Spain, Asia Minor, India and Sri Lanka.

STATUS OF TRUE CHAMELEONS

According to the regulations set forth by the Convention on International Trade in Endangered Species (C.I.T.E.S.), all true chameleons are listed as threatened under Appendix II. This means that special export permits are required from the country of origin for importation of chameleons into other countries.

UNDERSTANDING CHAMELEONS

True chameleons are lizards which have become specialized for living in shrubs, bushes and small trees. As a result they have evolved a **number** of adaptive features, some of which are unique among reptiles.

1. A laterally compressed body

Chameleons, depending on which species are involved, have bodies which are more or less laterally compressed (vertically flattened). Furthermore, all chameleons have some ability to vary the degree of lateral body compression through muscular action on the ribs for the purpose of thermoregulation, during movement and during territorial or aggressive displays.

A laterally compressed body will allow for relatively easy movement with minimal resistance among branches of tree and shrubs. In chameleons, it also allows for thermoregulation by allowing rapid heating when presenting a flattened side to the sun. This behavior is readily observed on cold morning or days. To reduce the rate of heating a chameleon can reduce the extent of flattening, and thus exposed surface area, by relaxing its rib muscles and by changing its position in relation to a heat source. However, if the ambient air temperature is too high, even after a chameleon has sought shelter in dense shade, chameleons can do little to cool down other than gape.

An additional feature of a laterally flattened body is that it can allow chameleons to avoid predators. A chameleon facing you while in a tree or shrub is very difficult to detect. Even if seen from the side by a possible predator, chameleons can at times remain so still that they are not easily detected. On the other hand, when approached or attacked by a potential predator, chameleons can display an extremely flattened and, when seen from the side, enlarged body. When combined with bright coloration and an-open mouth threat, this display can deter predators or animals seen as potential threats.

2. The ability to change color

Chameleons do not intentionally change color to match the surrounding environment but they may adopt colors and patterns which increase the probability of their blending with their surroundings. The ability of a chameleon to change color is limited to a range which is genetically programmed in a given species, population or individual. The ability to change color is also the result of adaptation to a life of living in trees or shrubs.

One function of color-changing ability in chameleons is to regulate body temperature. Unlike lizards that can find shelters underground when it is too warm or cool, chameleons remain exposed to the elements because of their specialized arboreal habits. Thus, a Jackson's chameleon which has remained all night in a bush may have been exposed to temperatures near freezing. When the morning sun first appears, it will present a flattened side to the sun and darken to nearly black because dark colors absorb more heat. Once it has warmed up it will lighten its color.

Color and pattern in chameleons also play a defensive role. When a potential predator is seen nearby, a chameleon may change to a highly patterned and multiple-contrasted color to increase the probability of its blending with a background and to visually break up its form. As the predator gets closer, and if the chameleon feels threatened, it may decide to adopt bright colors and vivid patterns to startle or dissuade a potential predator. Color also plays a significant role during intraspecies communication. Some of the most vivid colors are displayed by male chameleons confronting each other during territorial and aggressive displays. At that time, color and pattern becomes a way of signaling, "I'm an xxx chameleon species and I'm a male and do you want to challenge me?".

The above is a simplistic presentation of the role of color and pattern change in chameleons. For more information on the subject the reader is advised to research the scientific literature.

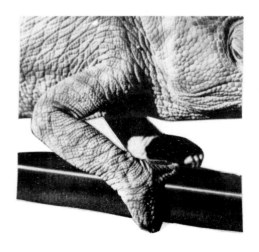

3. Specialized limbs and digits

Chameleons have evolved limbs of nearly equal length and digits that have fused to create pincer like claws that allow for easy movement in a three dimensional habitat.

4. A prehensile tail

True chameleons (with few exceptions) have a prehensile tail which can wrap around branches for stability while moving about in trees and shrubs. The tail of a chameleon is essential to its survival and not readily dispensable. Unlike most lizard species, chameleons cannot "drop" their tails when attacked by a predator, nor can they regenerate a tail if it were to be accidentally severed. In the wild, a chameleon which has lost part of its tail will usually not survive.

5. Fused eyelids and independent eye movement

The lids of the eyes of chameleons have become partially fused leaving only a small opening to allow light to reach the pupil. Only a very small section of iris is exposed. The eyes themselves can move independently allowing a chameleon to literally see two things at once if necessary (such as keeping an eye on a discovered insect prey while scanning with the other eye for possible predators) or focus together for acute binocular vision when aiming at prey.

6. A specialized tongue

Another remarkable feature of chameleons is the means by which they capture prey. Chameleons have the ability to project a specialized sticky-tipped tongue at a distance of more than twice their body length to capture an insect and retrieve it to the mouth. This capture method has co-evolved along with all the other specialized features of chameleons.

Chameleons, unlike other arboreal lizards, are incapable of the sudden dart and seize behavior that can be observed in most other arboreal insectivorous lizards. They have instead evolved the means of capturing prey at a distance while being able to depend on their essentially cryptic appearance.

The above information was presented so that the beginning herpetoculturist can develop an understanding and a "feel" for the special features and the needs of the chameleons he or she has an interest in keeping. This "feel" or "sense" will further develop as a result of observation and close attention to the clues expressed through a captive animal's behavior.

In the case of the husbandry of most chameleon species, so much information is lacking that adjustments will have to be made. Even within a given species of chameleon, varying populations of that species may have evolved adaptations to markedly different conditions and climate.

FACING THE FACTS ABOUT CHAMELEONS

Before deciding to get involved with keeping true chameleons in captivity, one has to consider these basic facts:

1. Several species of chameleons are difficult lizards to maintain long term in captivity. Many imported chameleons will die within six months of their importation because of internal parasites, disease and failure to acclimate. This is particularly true of the most commonly imported species at the time of writing, the Senegal chameleon *C. senegalensis*. On the other hand, some species are relatively easy to maintain when kept under the proper conditions (e.g. *C. jacksoni, C. johnstoni, C. oustaleti, C. pardalis and C. parsoni*).

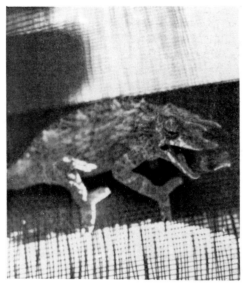

2. Most imported chameleons harbor parasites which should be treated to increase chances of survival in captivity. This will usually involve the cooperation of a veterinarian. Some specialized dealers now routinely treat imported chameleons for roundworms and some will even routinely treat them for protozoans. These dealers may be a good source for semi-parasite-free animals.

3. Success with true chameleons is labor intensive and involves daily care. They are not recommended for people who are too busy or who have

Male Johnston's chameleon (*Chamaeleo johnstoni*) which has just been hand fed a cricket coated with a paste wormer.

such large collections of reptiles or who are so diversified that they cannot focus on the care of these lizards. For a dedicated person willing to specialize with one group of lizards, chameleons are a good choice.

CHAMELEONS AS PETS

Under no circumstances should chameleons be considered as simply pets for children or adults. They require too much care and attention for successful maintenance and they resent any amount of handling or petting. Excessive handling or petting will contribute to the demise of chameleons due to stress. So kids ... LOOK BUT DON'T TOUCH.

Selecting Chameleons

This subadult female Johnston's chameleon *(Chamaeleo johnstoni)* would be a good initial selection for someone desiring to work with this species.

Selecting potentially healthy chameleons will be critical to your eventual success at maintaining these lizards. Do not for a minute have any notions of being a good samaritan and saving the poor thin, sickly lizard in a store. Sickly-looking chameleons almost always die. On the contrary, you should be extremely selective when choosing a chameleon for purchase and aim to select what appears to be a healthy and active animal. **The following are guidelines for selecting potentially healthy chameleons:**

A. A chameleon must show signs of alertness and activity when handled.

B. Its eyes must appear globular rather than sunken. When open, the eyelids must form a round opening rather than an elliptical one. The eyes must be active, indicating movement and alertness.

C. The specimen, when handled, must have a strong grip causing noticeable digital pressure on hand or object.

D. A chameleon must not be emaciated. The ribs and vertebral processes may be suggested but must not be prominently visible. The tail must be rounded and without the lateral depression indicative of poor weight and low fat reserves.

E. A chameleon must not show obvious signs of disease. It must have no unusual swellings on head, limbs or digits. When the mouth is open, no caseous material should be present in areas of teeth or gums. No red spotting should be present along the gums. Check the sides of the body for subcutaneous roundworms which will appear as coiled irregular masses beneath the skin. Avoid chameleons with these worms.

F. The specimen must not show signs of mites (body specked with white, powder-like deposits of crusty formations or tiny black or dark red specks crawling on body). Check the rims of the eyes of chameleons. When present, mites are commonly found lodged between the rim and the eye.

G. The color of a chameleon must be within the normal color range of the species and must indicate some capacity of adopting a darker coloration. The ability to change color can be considered an indicator of health. Unhealthy chameleons adopt either a uniformly dark or uniformly light coloration depending on species.

H. For the best chance of acclimating a chameleon to captivity select smaller and younger animals. These are usually more adaptable than large adults. Furthermore, since many chameleon species may be relatively short-lived, the probability of long term survival is significantly increased with smaller/younger animals.

I. Avoid females of egg-laying species which may be gravid (carrying eggs). Many of these tend to die while egg-bound or die following egg laying.

QUARANTINING

If you are keeping other chameleons, any new animal should be quarantined for at least six weeks in a room as far removed from your existing collection as possible. This will prevent the possible introduction of various diseases in your collection. In addition, some chameleons carry viruses which can wipe out members of a given species. The author has known two cases where entire breeding colonies of Jackson's chameleons died following the introduction of other animals. Following veterinary investigation, an airborne virus was suspected as the probable cause. Because considerable information is lacking on viruses that effect chameleons, you're better off being safe than sorry. **QUARANTINE NEW ANIMALS.**

9

Parasites

Most imported chameleons harbor large numbers of internal parasites which under the stresses of captivity often become a primary cause of the decline of a given animal. For anyone who decides to get involved with keeping chameleons, this is an issue which has to be confronted.

Ideally, one should consult a veterinarian specialized in reptile medicine and have at least a stool check and culture done. Realistically, most people will hesitate to spend money on veterinary services when the survival of an animal may be questionable anyway. So what should one do?

THE NEMATODE DILEMMA

Many species of imported chameleons harbor large numbers of nematode worms which under the stresses of captivity can become a primary cause of declining health and/or death. With most reptiles the solution would be relatively simple; administer the appropriate wormer. The problem with nematodes in chameleons is that they are not always in the G.I. tract. Several species of chameleons serve as intermediary hosts for worms that eventually migrate out of the G.I. tract and into areas beneath the skin. These "subcutaneous" nematodes are often visible in species such as *C. senegalensis, C. dilepis, C. gracilis and C. pardalis*. Often, only a small number of the worms present beneath the skin are visible. There can be many other "invisible worms" lying flat along the inner contours of the body.

Female panther chameleon *(Chamaeleo pardalis)* dissected by the author to expose subcutaneous nematodes.

10

In addition to the above, some species of chameleons may also harbor tiny nematodes called "filariae" and their larvae called "microfilariae" in the bloodstream. So what happens when you administer a wormer for treatment of nematodes? In some specimens, significant improvement in health and weight gain will follow within a few weeks of treatment. In some specimens, a period of stress and apparent illness will follow which may be accompanied by signs of internal bleeding including subcutaneous bleeding as well as swelling of digits and limbs. Some of these animals recover and do well, some die. Following treatment with a wormer, another possible outcome is a rapid decline within three days of worming which results in death.

Thus, a herpetoculturist is faced with a dilema. To worm a chameleon may kill it and not to worm a chameleon may kill it. Some chameleon species respond relatively well to worming because they seldom harbor nematodes that migrate under the skin. These would include *C. jacksoni, C. johnstoni, C. montium,* and *C. oustaleti.* But with other species, many factors may come into play including the geographical origins of given groups of imported animals. Some populations of a given species are less likely to be infected than others. So what does one do? **The following are possible approaches to this problem:**

1. Only buy small specimens of a given species and treat for worms. The underlying reasoning is that small animals which are younger are less likely to be heavily parasitized because they are less likely to have ingested large numbers of infected prey. If the means of infection were insect bites, younger chameleons would again tend to have a lower degree of infection.

2. With larger animals, monitor for several weeks before deciding to worm or not. If the animal loses weight in spite of regular feeding, have it checked for parasites and treat accordingly. If untreated, the animal would probably die anyway.

3. Treat all animals for nematodes. If they survive, great. If not then they probably would not have survived anyway. Getting rid of parasites will prevent possible infection of other established animals in a vivarium.

4. Avoid heavily parasitized species such as *C. senegalensis* and stick to other species which would then be routinely treated.

The decision as to what to do will ultimately be up to the individual herpetoculturist.

TREATMENT OF INTERNAL PARASITES

1. If the chameleons you have purchased were relatively expensive, then the cost of having a veterinarian check stool samples to determine the presence of various parasites is well justified as would be the cost of treatment. This would certainly be recommended with *C. pardalis, C. parsoni, C. melleri* and other expensive and large chameleons which would normally fare well in captivity. If your veterinarian is a specialist with reptiles, then having some blood tests may also be useful in determining the presence of parasites (e.g., microfilaria) as well as other types of infections.

2. One alternative which should be considered by specialized hobbyists, dealers and pet stores is to develop a program and routinely treat, with the cooperation of a veterinarian (as a source of medication and for determining proper dosage), all newly imported chameleons for roundworms and protozoans such as Trichomonas. Don't bother with stool cultures but use what some call a "shotgun" approach. This procedure has been criticized by some veterinarians but the truth of the matter is, that relatively inexpensive routine treatment can result in many more imported chameleons surviving. There must be a workable solution that allows for the treatment of high-risk, low-cost reptiles without the relatively expensive costs of veterinary treatment resulting in lack of treatment because "It is too expensive and it will probably die anyway".

The following are recommended treatments for newly imported chameleons:

For roundworms

Fenbendazole at a dosage of 50 mg/kg orally in a water solution via an eyedropper. Do not use a stomach tube. Repeat in two weeks.
     or
Levamisole hydrochloride at a dose of 5 mg/kg orally in a water solution via an eyedropper. Repeat in two weeks.
     or
Ivermectin - R
Use with caution. This is a very effective but touchy parasiticide. Some reptiles (e.g., turtles) have bad reactions to this drug and die. In other cases, some individuals react well to the drug while others do not. Veterinarians need to carry out well designed experiments on the use of Ivermectin in true chameleons. In the author's experience, some animals have no adverse effects to this drug while others go through a period of acute stress and others simply die. Species known to harbor large numbers of parasites including threadworms, such as *C. senegalensis*, often have adverse reactions possibly as a result of having to get rid of toxins associated with large numbers of dead parasite bodies. Recommended dosage: 200 mcg/kg orally. Repeat in two weeks.

12

For protozoans

Particularly *Trichomonas*, treat with Metronidazole at a dosage of 75 mg/kg administered orally. Repeat in two weeks.

OTHER PATHOGENS

Imported chameleons may harbor other pathogens which may require treatment, including coccidia (easily treated if detected early) and salmonella. One will require the cooperation of a veterinarian for the treatment of these diseases. It is best to have any cultures done while the animal appears healthy. By the time a chameleon demonstrates weight loss, sunken eyes and listlessness you may want to save your money. Sick-looking chameleons almost always die, with or without veterinary treatment.

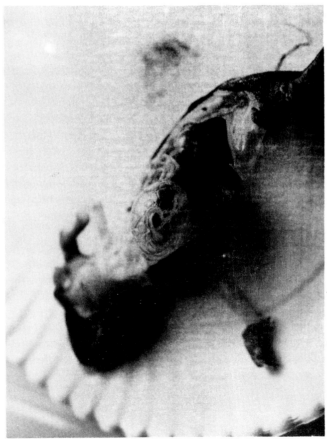

Note nematode worm embedded in lung tissue. The lungs of this female panther chameleon were expanded and contained bubbly mucus indicative of a respiratory infection. This species must be maintained at high temperatures to do well.

Acclimation

From the moment of capture, virtually all imported chameleons will have been subjected to varying degrees of stress. As a rule, imported animals are over-crowded, mishandled, underwatered and underfed, from the time they are trans-ported to holding compounds in the country of origin, to the time they arrive at the local pet store. Being aware of this, one must set out as quickly as possible to reduce stress and thus reduce susceptibility to disease.

The following are recommended procedures to acclimating newly imported chameleons:

1.   If an animal appears weakened and the eyes are partially sunken, administer an electrolyte solution with a plastic eye dropper. The solution can be purchased in the baby food section of supermarkets or drug stores. Gatorade® is an alternative to the electrolyte solution. Do not give too much at one time or the animal will choke and regurgitate. Administer twice daily. If an animal drinks on its own, use an electrolyte solution (not Gatorade ®) in a spray bottle. Rehydrating a chameleon is the most critical first step in acclimation.

2.   If the animal drinks on its own, spray the cage or gently spray the sides of a chameleon's mouth. Once it starts drinking, spray water gently into the mouth as it opens. Do this twice daily - morning and late afternoon.

3.   Put a chameleon by itself in a simple vivarium with branches and a plant. Cover the front of the vivarium so that the chameleon cannot see human activity which could elicit stress. Place a heat source which allows for basking. After a few hours, introduce two or three vitamin/mineral supplemented crickets.

4.   Keep the ambient temperature in the vivarium within the upper range of the animal's requirements. The immune system of reptiles becomes depressed at lower temperatures. At higher temperatures it becomes activated. An effective immune system will help the animal fight diseases and the effects of stress.

5.   Keep the chameleon under a normal photoperiod cycle.

6.   After a few days to a week, particularly if a chameleon appears more active and is feeding and drinking well, proceed with treatment for parasites if this is the course you have chosen.

14

Housing and Maintenance

NUMBER OF ANIMALS PER ENCLOSURE

Virtually all species of true chameleons fare best when kept singly within a given enclosure unless a very large and well landscaped enclosure is used. For breeding purposes, pairs can be maintained together for brief periods of time while keeping close observation as to the possibility of fighting. Some species, such as *C. jacksoni* and *C. hoehnelii*, can be kept in pairs in large enclosures while others, such as *C. africanus*, must always be kept singly outside of breeding attempts.

THE ENCLOSURE

This is the enclosed space which will contain the man-made chameleon microcosm.

TYPES OF ENCLOSURES

As a general rule, enclosures for captive Chamaeleo should consist of large cages. These can be made of wood or aluminum frame and hardware cloth or high quality plastic shade screening (preferred by the author). Sectioned off portions of rooms, or room-sized enclosures such as screen houses, aviaries or well ventilated greenhouses will also be suitable. As a second choice, very large, all-glass aquaria with appropriately designed extensions or lids have also been successfully used.

The author's outdoor chameleon screenhouse. The geese serve as guard animals against cats and possible trespassers.

SIZE OF THE ENCLOSURE

The following enclosure sizes are recommended for true chameleons:

For dwarf species (*C. bitaeniatus, C. ellioti, C. hoehnelii, C. lateralis, C. pumilus* etc.):
The recommended size is an enclosure 3 feet long x 18 inches wide x 2 feet high. Some herpetoculturists have been successful with standard 20 to 29 gallon aquaria with screen tops.

For medium to large species (*C. dilepis, C. jacksoni, C. johnstoni, C. senegalensis* etc.):
The enclosure should be at least 4 feet long x 2 feet wide x 4 feet high. Hobbyists have been successful with standard 29-gallon aquaria for individual animals and 40 to 55-gallon aquaria with screen tops for compatible pairs of given species.

For very large species:
The "giant" chameleon species; such as *C. oustaleti, C. parsoni* and *C. verrucosus*, should be housed individually either in enclosures at least 4 feet long x 2 feet wide x 4 feet high or in aquaria no smaller than a standard 55-gallon tank with a screen top.

In a room-sized enclosure, more than one male giant chameleon *(Chamaeleo verrucosus)* can be kept together. This is not a very agressive species.

BUT I JUST COULD NOT PASS IT UP...

What if, after entering a local pet store, you saw this chameleon that you "just had to have" and that you bought on impulse. It happens to many of us. But you just don't have the right type of enclosure and it could take days, even weeks before you can build or have built an adequate enclosure. Under certain circumstances, chameleons can be maintained successfully on large potted houseplants maintained in a room or screened patio that is bare enough that the animal(s) are easily located. Doors need to be kept shut to prevent escape as well as to keep out unwanted pets. Lights, heat sources, etc., will have to be placed in relation to the houseplants.

ADVANTAGES OF LARGE ENCLOSURES

The principal reasons large enclosures are recommended are as follows:

1.   They should be large enough to create, via spotlights and landscaping, a range of temperature and topographic conditions. This allows the chameleons to self-regulate their body temperatures and find suitable areas which provide them with the necessary physical and psychological comforts for survival in captivity.

2.   If a sexual pair or more than one species is kept together, they offer the topographic diversity to minimize territorial stress.

3.   It offers the space necessary for courtship and reproductive behavior.

LOCATION OF THE ENCLOSURE

The selection and location of a room or enclosure should, when possible, include a window with an eastern or southern exposure. This allows daily exposure to natural sunlight (through an open, screened window) and adequate air circulation (not draft). The inclusion of windows can also be useful in lowering natural temperature during cool months and, at various times of the year, in regulating environmental temperature (via opening or closing of window).

STRUCTURING THE SPACE WITHIN THE ENCLOSURE

With the exception of certain species of *Brookesia* , *Chamaeleo chamaeleo ssp.* and *Chamaeleo namaquensis* , most chameleons are primarily arboreal lizards having evolved a variety of physical and psychological specializations for life in a three-dimensional habitat (rocks, bushes and trees). **The habitat provides conditions which allow:**

a. thermoregulation via open-space basking areas and via shaded areas;

b. preferred resting areas and territory (preferred and defended activity area);

c. shelter from potential predators and excessive interspecies interaction; and

d. surfaces from which food and water can be obtained.

In the vivarium, these conditions are provided by placing dry tree branches and various live or artificial plants in relation to light sources, etc., in such a way that enough environmental variables are offered for an animal's needs to be fulfilled.

A STEP-BY-STEP DESIGN OF THE VIVARIUM

1. Select the right size vivarium and a suitable location for the vivarium.

2. Select a ground medium

In larger vivaria, the ground medium should consist of the ground or soil in which various plants will have been planted. In smaller vivaria, there are two alternatives. One is to use an easily replaced ground medium that allows for easy cleaning such as newspaper or brown paper. The other, is to use a layer of basic potting soil (without perlite that can be swallowed by lizards) over a one inch layer of pebbles for drainage. For gravid females, an area with at least six inches of potting soil should be provided in a secluded corner of the vivarium with overhanging plants and a slanted piece of cork above it. The use of moistened potting soil has the advantage of also raising relative air humidity in the vivarium.

3. Landscaping and topographic structuring of the vivarium

A. TOPOGRAPHIC STRUCTURING WITH DRY BRANCHES.

A number of dry tree branches should be carefully placed in the vivarium. A large proportion of the branches must have diameters within a range that allows for efficient gripping by the chameleon species maintained, (a diameter within a reasonable range of the combined inside measurement of two opposable digits). Somewhat smaller or larger is acceptable but too small can cause excessive local pressure between digits and too large (greater than twice the inside diameter) will not allow for an efficient grip. One should also avoid placing too many branches near each other (overly dense branches). These unnecessarily complicate the environment of these lizards making feeding, moving, shelter seeking and observation difficult.

The major consideration when placing branches is to carefully position them near windows and in areas where incandescent heat/light sources and full-spectrum lighting will be added. These branches will form the basking areas of the vivarium. Dry branches should also be placed in areas opposite the light sources, eventually to becoming the shaded areas and shelters of the vivaria. There should also be enough branches to create routes between basking and shaded areas for the specimen to move within broad areas (vertically and horizontally) of the enclosure. Branches should be placed in diagonal and near-horizontal positions rather than vertical positions.

B. SELECTION AND PLACEMENT OF LIVE OR ARTIFICIAL PLANTS.

Plants, either live or artificial, should be added to the vivarium for the following purposes:

 1. They will topographically structure the space within the vivarium in such a way that an animal will find preferred resting sites and shelters (from light) as well as establish a territory and movement routes.

 2. Plants also offer the necessary surface area for the settling of water droplets necessary to elicit drinking in chamaeleo species.

The plants must be placed in various relations to the dry branches to form shelters of vegetational clumps (leaves overhanging a branch), open areas and to provide leaves in close enough proximity to branches to allow drinking. The leaves of plants should not cover basking areas or be placed too close to directional heat/light sources (this will usually burn the plants). In addition, any newly purchased plant should be carefully washed to remove insecticidal residues. The plants can be placed directly in the ground medium or remain in pots depending on vivarium design.

The following live species have been used successfully by vivarists:
I. Trees useful in small sizes:
> *Ficus Benjamina*
> *Brassaia Species*
> *Scheffelera* (with large chamaeleo species only)
> and various citrus trees.

II. Trailing Philodendrons, Monstera, Pothos and other large vines.
These should be planted in the ground or in planters hanging from the wall of the vivarium. The vines should then be carefully arranged and anchored to dry wood or the vivarium frame to create the desired design.

Many other plant species can be used as long as they are branching and have small leaves. Plants that have elongated leaves (such as those of Dracaena or broad leaves (such as those of the rubber plant) should not be used.

Plastic artificial plants can also be used successfully as long as they are not composed of a toxic, leaching plastic. As with the selection or placement of branches, high-density levels of plants and/or leaves are not desirable. **The ideal chameleon environment offers numerous open areas as well as scattered shaded areas and shelters.**

19

Lighting

When maintaining chameleons in captivity three types of lighting are recommended:

    A.   Sunlight
    B.   Incandescent lighting
    C.   Full-spectrum lighting

SUNLIGHT

When possible, chameleons should be allowed to bask in direct unfiltered sunlight. This will provide U.V. radiation necessary for the synthesis of vitamin D and the absorption of calcium. Sunlight is also a good source of heat and has additional psychological as well as well as physical benefits which have not been determined. Accordingly, the author recommends exposure to an open eastern or southern window so the lizards can bask in unfiltered sunlight. During the warmer months of the year, chameleons can be placed outdoors in an appropriately designed screen enclosure to allow them the benefits of natural sunlight. These enclosures, in addition to an open area, should provide ample shade to permit the specimens to remove themselves from excess heat. Under no conditions should they be exposed to sunlight in glass or glass-sided containers since the Ultra Violet (U.V.) radiation will change to a lower frequency when passing through glass, at the expense of heat. The result is known as the "greenhouse effect". In a closed container, this could result in temperatures of 100F or more which will prove fatal to maintained specimens (Children, dogs and other animals have been killed when locked in a closed car exposed to the sun). An additional factor, is that sunlight filtered through glass will not offer the U.V. radiation required.

INCANDESCENT LIGHTING

In the vivarium, incandescent lighting is used primarily as a replacement for the directional heat radiation of sunlight. This is usually done by placing one or more spotlights over designated basking areas in such a way that the heat radiation and light is emitted at an angle rather than from above (as is usual in the design of most vivariums). Thus, a spotlight should be placed on a wall of the vivarium or angled from the ceiling. This is done to simulate sunlight as it occurs during the earlier and later hours of the day. In view of the information available on the basking behavior of chameleons, morning basking and a marked preference for lateral basking (presenting a single flatted side to the sun rather than the dorsum), suggests that this type of lighting design is more suitable for thermoregulation and more closely approximates the conditions of the natural habitat. Another form of basking behavior which the author has observed in gravid female chameleons involves ventral basking, literally presenting the ventral surface of the body to a directional heat/light source. This type of behavior is certainly unique among lizards and probably is due to the inability of these females to flatten the body laterally and to their relatively large ventral surface. It may play a significant role in the gestation rate and the even warming of developing embryos. The observation of this behavior has further reinforced the authors belief that chameleons have a marked preference for basking in a directional light source. It has also raised the possibility that lengthy gestations periods in captive females and possibly the birth of premature embryos may be related to an unsuitable basking site.

Female panther chameleon (Chamaeleo pardalis) "lateral basking" in the early morning following a cool night.

Placing incandescent lights

Spotlights are recommended over regular incandescent bulbs simply because they are more directional, concentrating more heat and light.

These spotlights should be placed in such a way that they illuminate the basking areas resulting in a temperature of between 85 degrees and 90 degrees farenheit when measured at the basking sites nearest to the bulbs. When placing these lights, special attention must be given to the following:

1. Spotlights should only be used with porcelain or other heavy duty light sockets capable of withstanding the heat produced.

2. They should not be placed in such a way that they are close to inflammable materials.

3. They should be placed in such a way that basking specimens cannot make direct physical contact with them and preferably at a distance of at least 18 inches from a basking site. Thermal burns, should they occur on chameleons, are usually fatal.

It is not possible to recommend specific bulb sizes. I personally find that 55 to 75 watt bulbs are adequate for large enclosures but the determining factors are distance from the basking site and the temperature of the basking site (between 85 and 90 degrees). In view of the ability of chameleons to raise their body temperatures above that of the air temperature (Burrage 1973) via basking behavior, this heat range will fulfill the thermoregulatory needs of most species.

On cold days, panther chameleons will sometimes bask on fallen trunks or rocks lying on the ground.

22

Inside of the author's chameleon screenhouse. Most chameleons are moved outdoors during the warm months so they can benefit from direct sunlight.

FULL-SPECTRUM LIGHTING AND BLACKLIGHTS

In recent years the use of full-spectrum lighting has been recommended for the rearing of many lizard species, particularly chameleons. From the point of view of vitamin D3 synthesis (the primary reason for which they are usually recommended) full-spectrum fluorescent bulbs are of questionable value since they generate little ultra violet radiation in the UVB range required for this process. On the other hand, full-spectrum bulbs may have beneficial psychological/behavioral effects and are therefore recommended for the successful maintenance of true chameleons. Blacklights, such as the General Electric F20T12, or the F40 BL by Sylvania ® that generate significant levels of UVA are also recommended when maintaining true chameleons indoors. The benefits of these bulbs is not related to vitamin D3 synthesis but to psychological and physical benefits attributed to UVA exposure. For the purpose of vitamin D3 synthesis, the best and safest method is to allow exposure to natural, unfiltered sunlight in a screened vivarium. If sunlight is problematical, one can resort to using a UVB Sun Lamp or Fluorescent Sun Lamp (FS-type) for no more than 10 to 20 minutes a day. However, no experimental work has been done on the use of these bulbs with the rearing or maintaining chameleons and one should use caution and carefully monitor the animals. These bulbs should be used with a shield to protect the eyes and skin of humans from exposure.

Temperature etc.

The issue of vivarium temperature with regard to the maintenance of chameleons has been a major concern of herpetoculturists. Ideally, one should attempt to gather as much information as possible on the species one is working with. With some species, information can be found in a university library with a good herpetology reference section. This will mean scanning the Zoological Record back several years and finding the specific references in herpetological journals. Relatively little in book form has ever been published on true chameleons. With other species, one may have to extrapolate from information obtained from an importer (who should at least know the animals' country of origin) and references on climate and habitats of various areas. This is not an easy task nor a very reliable one. Many species of chameleons are distributed over an extended geographical range resulting in populations adapted to different environmental conditions.

Another solution to the temperature problem, which tends to work well, is to determine suitable temperatures through experimentation and observation. This usually involves placing a chameleon in a vivarium with a range of temperature gradients and observing behavior. If the temperature is too high chameleons may show signs initially of hyperactivity followed by an obvious lightening of body color and eventually, by gaping of the mouth. Species that have a marked preference for cooler temperatures, will seek shade and descend to the ground under a shaded area.

When temperatures are too cool, a chameleon will spend marked amounts of time basking under a heat light while adopting a dark coloration. "Cold" chameleons will also not feed and tend to be listless. In the proper environment, chameleons tend to form specific behavior patterns in which part of the morning is spent basking, followed by an activity period which includes feeding. At midday, when the temperature is warmest, some chameleon species will continue to be active. Other species will seek shelters in the shaded areas but will emerge later in the day for activity and additional basking.

GUIDELINES FOR DESIGNING TEMPERATURE RANGES

For montane species, including egg-laying species such as *Chamaeleo montium* and most imported live-bearing species such as *C.bitaeniatus,C.helioti* and *C. jacksoni:*

Daytime temperature 70-80 degrees farenheit.
Basking area nearest to heat source 85F.
Nighttime temperature 60-70F but as low as 55F can be safely tolerated.

For most of the commonly imported egg-laying species:
Daytime temperature 80-88 degrees farenheit.
Basking area nearest to heat source 90F.
Nighttime temperature 65-78F.

Recommended methods for temperature regulation

The daytime temperatures indicated can be obtained via room heaters if necessary. In most homes these temperatures are close enough to average room temperatures that they will be raised by the light sources in the vivarium.

For cooling a vivarium during the warm summer months, one method is to use a drip or mist system on a timer which will cool by evaporation if combined with the use of a fan. This method has its limits. It will not be efficient for cooling montane species when ambient temperature is greater than 90F. At extreme temperatures, the only solution is to bring the animals indoors in an air conditioned room. At other times of the year the temperature can often be lowered by simply opening a window to varying degrees depending on outside daytime or nighttime temperatures.

AIR HUMIDITY

In his Royal Natural History published in 1896, Lydekker pointed out an interesting aspect of the distribution of chameleons. He stated: "Like most of the Malagasy compatriots, the lemurs, chameleons are chiefly found only in regions where foliage is abundant and where the fall of rain and dew is sufficient to supply them with the amount of moisture they need. Consequently they are most numerously represented in coast districts and islands. A few, however, frequent such parts of desert regions which come under the influence of sea moisture and support a more or less scanty vegetation." Thus the dependence of chameleons on air humidity, primarily as a source of water (dew, fog), had been recognized by early naturalists. More recent works have further confirmed this point of view. They have also indicated that, in addition to providing the chameleon's principal source of water, air humidity may play a significant role in reducing the rate of dehydration.

In the vivarium, since water is usually supplied by means other than condensation of air humidity (dew), air humidity plays an insignificant role in providing water to captive specimens. However, air humidity appears to play a significant role in terms of dehydration rates. Newly imported specimens showing symptoms of dehydration tend to improve faster when water is administered in combination with the use of a cool-air humidifier. Chameleons should be maintained at a 50 to 60% average relative humidity level in well ventilated enclosures. With montane and forest species, and when rearing juveniles of these species, the use of cool-air humidifiers or evaporative coolers can be beneficial. When using cool-air humidifiers they should be placed in such a way that the animals can move away from the spray. For obvious reasons, adequate ventilation is essential.

AIR CIRCULATION

A vivarium containing chameleons should have good air circulation provided either through the use of a small fan blowing the air out of the vivarium or, better yet, through the use of a partially opened window. Small fans that can easily be integrated within the top of a vivarium can be purchased through electronic supply stores. A screen must be used to prevent any possible contact with the fan. **The benefits of air circulation are:**

1.   It prevents the build up of heat in the vivarium and thus allows for the establishment of the temperature gradients required for the maintenance of these lizards.

2.   It prevents bacterial and fungal growth which could occur in a situation where stagnant air is combined with high humidity, relatively high temperature and low light levels (in the shaded areas of vivariums).

One should, of course, not confuse good air circulation with drafts; air circulation implies air exchange in the environment and drafts implies air current. Drafts should be avoided in the chameleon vivarium. A draft leads to rapid evaporation of water within the vivarium and can increase dehydration of animals.

Gravid female Johnston's chameleon (Chamaeleo johnstoni) in a sheltered area of vivarium.

Feeding

Proper feeding of true chameleons is critical to their survival for any length of time in captivity. In fact, feeding is the most time consuming task one has to perform in the daily maintenance of these lizards. **When feeding chameleons, the following issues have to be addressed:**

1. Selecting food items that may be nutritionally adequate and that the chameleon will be interested in capturing.

2. Feeding a varied diet usually consisting of commercially-raised crickets as a staple supplemented with varying amounts of other insect species.

3. Boosting the nutritional value of the diet through nutrient loading of insects and vitamin/mineral supplementation.

4. Offering the diet in a manner that minimizes food dispersal (such as fast escape by insects) and reduces the rate at which supplements are lost.

SELECTING FOOD ITEMS

All chameleons identify potential food items visually. Thus, any potential prey must display characteristics and behaviors that elicit capture and feeding behaviors. For chameleons, size of insect, movements that an insect makes while remaining in place, amount of glistening (light reflected by shiny parts of the body), as well as form and color can play a role in a chameleons decision to capture prey.

For chameleons kept in captivity the selection of potential insects will be in part limited by their availability. For obvious reasons commercially produced insects that are readily available should be the primary selections for feeding chameleons. **The following are insects that are recommended for feeding chameleons in captivity:**

Gray crickets, *Acheta sp.*
These are available in a variety of sizes from pinheads to large, winged adults. They can be obtained through specialized pet stores and through commercial breeders who sell them by mail order for bait. For most chameleon species these will be a dietary staple because of relatively low chitin content (particularly in immature animals which lack wings) and because they can easily be nutritionally boosted and vitamin/mineral supplemented.

Mealworms, *Tenebrio*

As a staple diet these are unsuitable for chameleons primarily because of high chitin content and because they are nutritionally deficient. Nonetheless, in a varied chameleon diet, occasionally offering a small number of mealworms of the right size, particularly just molted "white mealworms", will add variety to the diet.

King mealworms, *Zoophobias*

Larger than standard mealworms. These appear to be better than regular mealworms for feeding chameleons. Depending on size and species they can be used in varying amounts in the diets of medium to large chameleons. "White", just-molted *Zoophobias* can be used with most species while chitinized worms are best with larger species. When offered in small numbers (1 to 2 every other feeding for medium chameleons) they can help fatten up chameleons. Giant species such as *C. parsoni* can often be started on *Zoophobias*. These can safely constitute a significant proportion of their diets. Otherwise, same information as for mealworms applies.

Wax worms, *Galleria melonella*

These are the caterpillars of waxmoths. They can be obtained via mail order fish bait businesses and through pet dealers who specialize in reptiles. Many chameleon species will take these readily. As a dietary item they can be used to supplement a diet based on crickets but should not be used as a basic diet. They are nutritionally deficient and tend to be high in fat. Unlike crickets and mealworms, they cannot readily be nutrient loaded. These are best used as a small component in a varied chameleon diet.

Chilean caterpillars, *Chilecomodia moorei*

These colorful red or yellow caterpillars resemble giant wax worms. They are available only in a few areas and are just now being considered for possible distribution in the pet trade. They are relished by many chameleon species. *C. parsoni* will readily feed on them. Like wax worms, these are probably best used as a small component in a varied diet.

Roaches

Because of their bad reputation as holusehold pests, cockroaches are not usually considered as a potential food source for chameleons. It would, however, be a mistake to disregard them. There are several tropical species that are offered via biological supply houses that cannot climb glass (can be raised in an aquarium) and that will not establish in American households if they were to escape. A good choice is *Blaberus craniiferus*, obtainable from some of the large biological supply houses. For several species that may be reluctant to feed on crickets (e.g., *Chamaelo parsoni*), cockroaches can often provide the stimuli that elicit feeding.

Wingless fruit flies

These can be obtained through biological supply houses and through breeders who advertise in tropical fish magazines under "Live Foods". They are a useful back-up source (when pinhead to week-old crickets are not available) for raising hatchling or newborn chameleons.

Flies

For a number of reasons, including the fact that they may be disease carriers and that they are often nutrient deficient, the author does not recommend flies as a chameleon diet.

Mice

Some of the larger chameleons will take "pink " (newborn to 1 week old) mice, the very large species *C. parsoni, C. verrucosus* will even take "fuzzy" (unweaned mice with closed eyes and hair just beginning to appear) mice.

NUTRIENT LOADING OF INSECTS

A common saying nowadays is "You are what you eat", but when one considers predators like chameleons that feed on whole prey, a more appropriate saying would be "You are what your prey eats".

Indeed, when a chameleon eats an insect, it not only has available the nutrients that make up the insect itself, but also the nutrients that the insect harbors in the form of undigested plant and animal matter stored in its gut. In nature, any consumed insect will provide these "stored" nutrients and one cannot think of a proper chameleon diet without considering what this stored food may provide.

Crickets with pinched off hindlegs in a porcelain sauce dish with added vitamin/mineral supplement.

This may be nature's way of making sure that a chameleons gets its "veggies" along with whatever vitamins they may supply.

It is questionable that the crickets or mealworms you buy at a pet store have high nutritional value. Many pet stores do not bother to feed their insects and, if they do, the feeding and watering will not provide a high quality nutrition. So, one of the tasks of any chameleon keeper will be to nutritionally boost food items prior to feeding their chameleons. One way, of course, would be to raise one's own insects but that is not practical for most people. The easiest is to have a couple of plastic terrariums in which purchased insects will be nutritionally boosted prior to being fed to chameleons.

A standard procedure for nutritional boosting of crickets, mealworms and roaches is to keep the insects with no food or water for one day so that they clear their guts of any food previously eaten and also so that they become hungry. Then offer, after 24 to 36 hours, a finely ground "rodent chow" or monkey chow with calcium carbonate or OsteoForm ® mixed in. The food should be in nearly powder form. This can be done by using a hammer after placing food between layers of brown paper (such as that of shopping bags) or in a food processor.

As a source of water use slices of oranges that will provide vitamin C and alternate with grated carrots, which will provide vitamin A. Do not use potatoes as a source of water, as recommended by cricket breeders.

Offer insects the day after the insects have been nutrient loaded.

Roaches
Use same procedure as above.

Mealworms
Use same procedure as above but, instead of oranges place pieces of carrots as a source of water.

VITAMIN/MINERAL SUPPLEMENTATION

Prior to feeding, all insects should be coated with a powdered vitamin/mineral supplement consisting of a mix with two parts of a high-quality bird or reptile multi-vitamin/mineral supplement and one part calcium carbonate. Better yet is OsteoForm ®, a calcium supplement that also supplies the right phosphorus ratio as well as D3. This can be obtained through a veterinarian or select feed stores or, increasingly, pet stores which specialize in reptiles. To apply the supplement, place a teaspoon or two of the mix in a jar, add insects and shake gently.

Note:
To reduce the rate of escape of crickets, it is recommended that their hind (jumping) legs be pinched off. This can be done by pinching the "thigh" section of the leg which the crickets will then usually drop. This is not necessary in pinhead to two week-old crickets. (See next section).

Pink mice
Pink mice have poorly developed skeletons and thus are calcium deficient as a lizard diet. Dip the rump of a pink mouse in calcium carbonate or OsteoForm ® prior to offering them to chameleons.

THE RIGHT WAY TO OFFER FOOD TO CHAMELEONS
Many people, when feeding all insect-eating lizards, have the bad habit of just throwing insects in the enclosures. In the case of chameleons many escape, others are caught later after most of the vitamin/calcium supplementation has come off. The right way to feed chameleons is to devise systems that regulate or restrict food dispersal.

One system is to create a platform or other means of hanging a porcelain bowl or smooth, plastic bowl in which the insects are placed. The legs of crickets should have been pinched off prior to coating with a supplement. With this kind of system the insects cannot climb out and escape from the smooth/slick-sided bowl. More than one bowl may be necessary so that the food items are within range of the field of vision of the chameleon.

An alternative is to use a strategically placed feeding tube or feeding container with a hole or two at the bottom and space to add a vitamin/mineral powder so that the insects come out of the holes fully coated. Chameleons will eventually learn to feed from the containers. As a back up, place a large porcelain bowl underneath so that food that escapes is trapped in the bowl.

HAND-FEEDING
One of the best methods for feeding chameleons is to hand-feed them. This consists simply of holding a live prey item such as a cricket or king mealworm between the thumb and index finger and presenting it within striking distance of a chameleon. With this method, you can maintain control on the amount of food as well as the type of food ingested and reduce significantly the loss of any supplement. Many species and individual chameleons will feed readily from the hand if one stands relatively still during the process. Eventually, chameleons can become conditioned to this type of feeding and will even learn to take dead prey.

Another advantage to this type of feeding is that it can allow you to medicate your animals simply by using crickets or other foods as a vehicle for administration. The author when worming his chameleons simply applies the appropriate amount of worm paste to a cricket and hand feeds the specimens that will take food in this manner.

Male panther chameleo (Chamaeleo pardalis) having just seized a cricket form the author's hands. This is a very effective and controlled manner of feeding chameleons.

FEEDING SCHEDULES

As with most reptiles, feeding schedules should vary depending on the age of the animal. A feeding schedule should correlate to some degree with growth rate. During the period of high growth rate, from juvenile to adult (a 100-fold or more increase in weight in medium to large chameleon species), food should be offered more frequently to supply the nutrients, vitamins and minerals to build the fast growing skeletal and muscular systems. Once the animals have reached adult size, feeding should be adjusted depending on whether the animal is being conditioned for breeding, whether the animal will be kept as a single display, and/or if the animal is showing signs of possibly becoming obese.

For all species of chameleon

From a hatchling or a newborn juvenile (in live bearing species) to an adult size (at which point growth rates tapers drastically and appears to level off), offer food twice a day and up to three times a day. Ideally, you want juveniles to grow as quickly as possible. Underfed juveniles will become stunted and will not usually survive. For chameleons and many other reptiles, the first six months of growth will determine whether you end up with large or stunted adults. Many species of chameleons will reach sexual maturity at 12 to 18 months. When you compare the size of a newborn Jackson's chameleon to that of a young adult, you will realize what a phenomenal growth rate this is. A human being has around a twenty-fold increase in weight from birth to the age of 19.

Adults

Feed every one to two days. Wild-caught animals, such as Senegal chameleons which harbor parasites, may have to be fed daily to maintain body weight, but once deparasitized, you will notice that adult chameleons such as Senegals will maintain body weight on a four-times-a-week feeding schedule. Females to be conditioned for breeding or females that have just layed eggs or given birth should be fed more frequently. Use your common sense.

WATER

Most imported chameleons arrive in a dehydrated state and regular availability of water is critical during acclimation as well as in the course of regular maintenance. Chameleons, however, will not readily drink from water dishes that contain still water. They are attracted to and drink from droplets of water that reflect light. They are also drawn to water droplets trickling down a leaf or other surface. **The following are some of the methods used by herpetoculturists to water chameleons.**

Spray bottles

This is the most commonly used method for watering chameleons. Water is sprayed from a spray bottle onto leaves of plants and walls of the vivarium so a chameleon can drink from the droplets. Another approach is to gently spray the head of a chameleon until it begins drinking movements of the mouth and then gently spray directly in their mouth. The main problem with this method is that water becomes available only when you are spraying. Another problem is that you risk soaking the vivarium in the process and causing the ground medium to become drenched with water.

Air pump system

This watering method is relatively simple, it consists of a small aquarium air pump placed outside of the vivarium with an air hose leading into a water dish. Branches carefully positioned around the water dish allow a chameleon ready access to the glimmering water and surrounding droplets. Problems with this system can include soaking the surrounding area and a high rate of water evaporation from the dish.

Intravenous drip system

An intravenous drip obtained from a medical supply store is placed over the top of the vivarium with drops set to fall at a regular rate over a given section of plants and branches. Underneath the drip, a flat pan is set to collect excess water as it falls. The advantage to this system is the long-term continuous availability of dripped water with the regular trickle of water down leaves or other surfaces. The disadvantage is the risk of soaking the vivarium if the system is not well designed.

Pipette watering

Watering with a pipette by first putting a few drops over the head and then administering water directly into the mouth, is another method used by some herpetoculturists. As a watering method, this is primarily recommended for administering vitamins or medications in a more controlled manner but without causing the stress of handling.

WATERING SCHEDULE

Water **at least** once daily and preferably **twice daily.**

A commercial screen and mylar reptile cage is ideal for chameleons. Some stores in Southern California now sell these cages. Note the simple watering system: a deli container with water dripping out of a hole punched in the botton onto the leaves of a plant and into the lower deli cup.

Conclusion

We are now on the verge of many breakthroughs in herpetoculture in terms of diet, lighting, heating systems, vivarium design and herpetological medicine. The development of the body of knowledge now known as herpetoculture will continue unless animal welfare agencies, such as the Humane Society of America, succeed in their constant endeavor to sponsor and propose legislative regulations that would prohibit the private sector from keeping exotic animals, including reptiles.

As herpetoculturists we must strive to practice responsible herpetoculture that further contributes to that body of knowledge and that emphasizes long-term self-sustaining captive breeding populations. True chameleons are species whose collection in the wild should be managed (they could become a significant economic resource for Madagascar) and whose importation should be regulated through a quota system to prevent over-collection, with controls to assure proper treatment and packing at the time of shipping. The survival of several species of true chameleons is now threatened as a result of habitat destruction. We can sit back and hope that conservationists and zoos will take care of their conservation...or as herpetoculturists, we can work on solving the herpetoculture of these species while they are still available. A key to success will be perseverance in spite of failures and the willingness to experiment with and modify vivarium design, temperature variables and diet.

The position advocated by some herpetoculturists that chameleons are so difficult to keep that they should not be imported is not warranted considering the increasing successes with several of the Madagascar species such as *C. pardalis*. What we should all strive for, instead of advocating defeatist and negative positions, is to pursue in a methodical and responsible manner, herpetocultural research that strives to elucidate problems of the husbandry and propagation of reptiles.

Now also available:
The General Care and Maintenance of True Chameleons, Part II: Notes on Popular Species; Diseases and Disorders by Philippe de Vosjoli.

Source Materials

Burrage, B.R. 1973. " The ecology of Chamaeleo namaquensis and Chamaeleo pumilus". Annals of the South African Museum. (Vol. 61).

Bustard R. 1989. Keeping and Breeding Oviparous Chameleons. British Herp. Soc. Bul. No 27.

De Vosjoli, P. 1979. "The care, maintenance and breeding of the African Chamaeleo". Chameleon Research Center. Journal #2 pp. 7-42.

De Vosjoli, P. 1990. The Right Way to Feed Insect-eating Lizards. Advanced Vivarium Systems. Lakeside, CA.

Frye, F.L. 1981. Biomedical and Surgical Aspects of Captive Reptile Husbandry. Veterinary Medicine Publishing Company, Kansas.

Obst, F.J., Richter, K., and Jacob, V. 1988. The Completely Illustrated Atlas of Reptiles and Amphibians for the Terrarium. T.F.H.

Shifter, H. 1984. "Chameleontidae" in Grzimek's Encyclopedia of Animal Life. Vol. 6. Reptiles. Van Nostrand Rheinhold. N.Y. pp. 227-241.